HOW TO BE A GOOD WIFE

A Simple Guide That Every Bride Need To Know

Emmanuel Aniekan

Copyright

Copyright ©2020, Emmanuel Aniekan.

Disclaimer

Though, I ensured the information in this book was correct and accurate as at the time of writing, I cannot guarantee with certitude that it will remain so because of how technology evolves and the dynamic nature of the internet.

Also, the advice and recommendation in this book are based on my experience and this may change due to circumstances beyond my control.

However, I'll try to update this book when such situation occurs and Amazon will send you a **free** copy to keep you apprised.

Emmanuel Aniekan

But the nature of my busy schedules might cause a little delay because I'm really not **"The Flash"**.

INTRODUCTION

I want to talk about how a wife keeps a good husband and I emphasize on a "good husband" covered.

I'm using the word: "good husband" covered intentionally because just like the husband the man covers the wife, the wife also covers the man as well.

She covers him from a lot of the things. Just like the emphasis made in *Proverbs 31* where the woman did her husband such good that he had no need of spoil.

In other words, she covered him in all bases and this is important in the life of a wife and in the life of a family.

A man needs a wife that will cover him in all bases and that's what I want to deal with in this book.

So, what are some of the mistakes that wives makes as it relates to a good husband.

I'm emphasizing that because a lot of times a guy that is not even a husband much less a good husband believes that he is worthy of such submission and he is worthy of offerings of honor and the steam from his wife but a man has to first be a husband.

Adam had to exist before Eve could even come into existence. God pulled Eve out of Adam which means if you're going to be the head, you've to be the head in all things.

Again, I'm emphasizing a good husband because there are a lot of ladies or women who have good husbands and the reality is that you're not covering that man.

In other words, you're not handling that man properly as he needs to be handled.

If you think about it when you had men that dishonored you or when you had men that abused you or when you had men that would not commit to you or would not marry you but you gave them the world and then when God blesses you with the man that he may not be perfect because none of us are when God blesses you with a man that honors you enough to marry and is trying to do his best to be a good husband quite often he gets the raw end of the deal.

It seems you kind of make him pay for all of the men that didn't and if you really pay attention to the way you handle your good husband, you're giving him less than you gave the men that abused you and I believe somebody needs to sound the alarm because I see a lot of marriages that are being wrecked because wives quite honestly just are not wise.

I need you to understand what I'm saying to you and that's why I'm emphasizing a good husband if you have a good husband you should not have any argument against the stuff that I'm going to talk about in this book.

In the book of **Genesis chapter 2 verses 24 – 25**, it says: *"Therefore shall a man leave his father and his mother, and shall cleave unto his wife and they shall be one flesh. And they were both naked, the man and his wife, and we're not ashamed."*

In that chapter above, it says therefore shall a man leave his father and his mother which means that in other for a man to be a good husband, he has to makes his wife a top priority.

In other words, if we're to define a good husband, we would say a good husband makes his wife his priority.

His friends are not his priority neither is his work. His ministry is not his priority.

His mom and dad are not his priorities, (they should be a priority but they are not his number-one priority), his children are not his number-one priority.

When a man has a good wife and the bible says in that same **Genesis chapter 2 verses 24**...*leave your father and* *mother*, it's speaking of making the wife his priority. If you've a husband that makes you the priority, you're blessed.

Then still on the same **Genesis chapter 2 verses 24**, it still goes on to say *…and shall cleave unto his wife…* which means that not only does he make her the priority but cleave means to stick to her like glue.

It now means that he pursues his wife. In other words, he's in constant pursuit of his wife and his wife is never feeling like she's invisible to him.

He's always in constant pursuit of his wife, he loves his wife's company, he longs to be in his wife's company, and no one else has his attention.

In other words, he pursued her to get her after he has attained her and they are married, he still pursues her the same way it says in: **Genesis chapter 2 verses 24 – 25:** *…shall a man leave his father and mother and cleave unto his wife. And they were both naked the man and his wife and were not ashamed.*

He should protect his wife for her to be naked and not be ashamed means that she was secure when there were no insecurities about our surrounding Adam.

She was totally secure in his presence physically and emotionally as well as spiritually.

A woman should be able to be naked before her husband and feel totally secure because he has to be her place of protection.

So as a husband, you have to ask yourself: is my wife really my number-one priority? Am I really in pursuit of my wife? Do I really go out with my wife like I did before we got married and does my wife feel safe in my presence? Does she feel protected? Can she be naked and not ashamed?

In the book of **Proverbs chapter 14 verses 1** it says: *"Every wise woman buildeth her house but the foolish plucking it down with her hands.* That's proverbs 14 and 1 every Wise Woman builds her house but the foolish plucking it down with her hands.

If you are not wise as a wife, you can destroy your own family. Yes, that's not a typo: you can destroy your own home.

You can have a great husband and if you're not functioning in wisdom, you can destroy your marriage and your family with your own hands.

If you've paid attention to anything relative to men, you would have noticed that men are internalized.

What that means (quite often it does not make it right but it's real quite often) is that your husband can feel humiliated, neglected, unappreciated, and internalize which explains why this is very important.

If a wife does not feel prioritized, pursued, and protected. These are the things that a woman is really talking about when she says I shouldn't have to tell you this because she feels like this should be a natural outflow of your manhood likewise when a woman doesn't know how to handle a good man properly quite often he does not know how to articulate what he's feeling so he internalizes it and by the time you discover it, you've broken your man.

And most times, you would have broken him beyond the point of repair and lease in his mind and that's exactly what I'll be sharing in this book.

Though, it may come across as harsh but I need you to kind of take it and digest it and think about it even those of you that are not married but are thinking about getting married or are engaged, these are certainly some things that you need to think about as a wife because these are the things that I'm going to list in this book.

These things are important to a man especially when he's a man that is doing his part regarding providing for the family.

There are some things that he expects you as his wife to understand and to know and to fulfill as well in his life. Which is similar to the instruction (regarding covering him) in the book of **Proverbs 31** where the *woman did her husband so good that he had no need of spoil.*

My wife keeps me covered on all levels and that's why I encourage brothers to wait for the right one because you need a woman that can really hold you down.

Our husbands can become disgusted because of the wife's sensual stupor.

The wife's sensual stupor is the spirit of apathetic sensuality in the life of a wife that quite often destroys her man's core.

What does all of that fancy language mean?

It means that as a wife, you cannot allow yourself to get to the point where you become so familiar and you take things for granted and everything becomes a routine with you.

You get to the point where you never give your man the kind of sex appeal that attracted him and it's amazing how you know and I see it all the time jokingly but in a lot of instances, it is really not a joke.

It's amazing how you go to the altar (and I say the wedding day is the biggest day of false advertisement) and the woman is just looking like a dream and quite often that's the first and last time you're going to see a look like that which is not supposed to be so.

Well, that'll not to be the case with wives when God has joined you in union with a man you have to understand that man needs you to keep him stimulated.

You cannot allow yourself to just fall off because now you're married: you got the ring and now you just let yourself fall off by not taking care of yourself.

You have to make certain that you keep your man covered. A man is visual and is in constant need of visual and physical stimulation.

Now, let me bring some balance to this of course, when your marriage have children and you work in a job, it would be unrealistic for a man to think you're going to be putting it on like that every day because that's just inhumane.

It's definitely not going to happen but quite honestly, you shouldn't allow just weeks to pass by before you give your man something to think about and I'm trying to keep this social media friendly, you know at least once every seven days he ought to see.

Do you know why the strip clubs are always packed? As you're reading this book, strip clubs are packed and a lot of those guys are married for several years. So, why are they throwing their money on the stage to look at a woman that's not theirs?

Most of the time, it's because when they go home, their wives have become so disconnected, disinterested, and indifferent about her sex appeal towards her husband.

Isn't it amazing how when you're single, you can put it on all the time for men that are not even supposed to necessarily behold all of that and then you get married and you lose all of that?

Again, get this straight: I'm emphasizing on a good husband because I wouldn't want all the ladies coming after me after reading this book.

How is it that you can't put yourself together and turn your sexy on for a good husband when you used to do that for your men?

You'd have your stuff together and get your hair right, nightwear on, playing for your man and now that you got a husband that's working, loving, going to church, raising the children, taking care of your honor in you and you mean this man can't come home and expect that his wife is going to be looking good?

Come on!

Everybody wants a wedding but not everybody wants to be married. There's a difference between the wedding and the marriage. And what I'm talking about is marriage.

As a husband, you've to make your wife your top priority. You've got to pursue your wife like you got a data which you did consistently before you got married so she got to feel safe in your care. She got to feel protected.

He needs you to step out or get outside of your sensual stupor just like what the Bible says in **1 Corinthians chapter 11 verses 7**: *"For man indeed ought not to cover his head for as much as he is the image and glory of God but* *the woman is the glory of the man."*

And that term glory means that she's the dignity, honor, and praise a man finds.

Now, when I read this: it leads me into saying that it's important for you to put yourself together as his wife especially when you're going out publicly.

This is important because a man finds his greatest pride in the condition of his wife and it speaks volume of the kind of care you husband is dispensing.

For example, you shouldn't be allowing your hair all over the place or wearing colors that don't match and all those kind of things that's makes you look dated and unattractive.

The main testament to the man's social and psychological success as a man is the quality of woman he has on his side.

Now, why is the woman's sensuality towards a man important?

Listen to this very carefully: the woman's sensuality towards her husband is important because her sensuality is the testament to his place in her life and heart.

He has to know even though it is probably more frequent that the man initiates sensual activity, he has to feel that his wife desires that kind of activity.

He should never come in the house and feel like you don't want to engage him sexually or romantically because a real man if he feels that he doesn't know that you desire him in that fashion, he'll just suppress that part of his nature.

He's not going to push himself upon you and even if he's married to you, if you don't project that I desire you therefore I make myself desirable to you.

I hope you're getting what I'm pointing out in this book so far. When a wife cares nothing about her appearance or sex appeal, it computes in the man's mind as a direct rejection of himself.

For example, if I'm coming home every night and my wife's hair is all over her head and she's coming to sleep with sweat suits on.

In other words, she's not taking care of herself and if I know it's no financial matter.

And I come home constantly and she looks a wreck at some point in my masculine psychology that is going to say to me that she is now rejecting me.

It's important for you to communicate to your husband that you desire him by making yourself desirable.

This is one of the areas where you know the female brain and the male brain are different because a woman is moved by what they in turn.

Of course, women loves the way a man looks but the reality is that a lot of beautiful women have married ugly dudes because he had a good heart and he knew what to say and so a woman is typically moved by a man's heart and what comes out of him while a man is attracted to a woman primarily by what he sees.

If he's a wise man, he learns to engage her soul in a spirit and all that kind of thing but it does not eliminate the fact that he needs to see something and a wife that is wise keeps herself in a place where she is sexually appealing to her husband.

After a man has been married to one woman for so long, it takes more than the presence of a disrobe body to reach him.

The man is built for intrigue which is why he will stand in the freezing cold and wait to kill an animal that is running for his life which is similar to the intrigue a hunter has.

The average wife will devote herself to her kids, her job, her career, business etc and still come home and give her husband the five percent left over.

After long periods of neglect, this creates a deficiency in the male psyche and leaves him vulnerable to the many forces of everyday existence.

So, you can have your career and children but if you don't take care of the foundation, your marriage is a recipe for failure.

The wise wife reinvents herself sensually for her husband.

A wise wife will learn to dress for her husband but unfortunately, most wives dressed to impress the other sisters and people in the world but every wise woman that wants to keep her husband fascinated will definitely dress for him especially at bedtime.

Let's have a look at what the **Song of Solomon chapter 4**

verses 11 says: *"Thy lips, O my spouse, drop as the honeycomb: honey and milk are under thy tongue; and the smell of thy garments is like the smell of thy garments is like the smell of Lebanon."*

In other words, women ought to have fragrances to keep her smell nice and attractive and you should always ask your husband what he would like to see you wear.

As a wife, you have to take the time to stimulate your husband especially as he gets older.

Once, the man gets past 50, he literally has to be stimulated because as he gets older his body changes and so now his mind has to communicate to his body that it's time to go and so he needs to be stimulated and if this isn't done, you cause some things to die in him.

His manhood will die because his woman is no longer stimulating it and if his wife is no longer stimulating that part of his life, he's consumed with what children and financial future demands.

Once you've allowed that part of him to die and that is your job as his wife to make certain that he keeps his eyes on you and that he has no reason to stray but more importantly that you keep that part of his manhood stimulated.

He needs to connect the sexual aspects of his manhood to his wife and he needs to view you sexually.

Another hindrance to marital bliss is when the wife constantly fights against the man's position of headship.

When a man has to constantly battle his wife off the pants, it throws the divine order of the family and it also confuses the chemistry.

Both of you are in Dominion and you know that's what I teach when we start talking about the wife submitting but that does not mean that she is a second-class citizen.

Emmanuel Aniekan

You're cold dominators but you have specific roles in the kingdom dynamic of the family and it doesn't necessarily mean that the man is always making the decisions because in most families that I know that work well.

When the man is married to a competent woman, he allows her to make most of the decisions.

In my house, my wife makes most of the decisions to be honest with you especially when I got so much going on.

For example, I didn't want to live in Texas but my wife came and said that's exactly where we should stay and she went ahead to buy the house.

The place I wanted to go live flooded the place I submitted to her so she said she won't live high and dry.

So, when we start talking about submission, don't get it twisted because it doesn't mean that the man is the boss and you're the slave.

That's just a misappropriation of facts but no man wants a wife that he has to fight when he says this is the direction I think we need to go in.

If this man is prioritizing you, pursuing you, protecting you, and honoring you and he says this is the way he think you want to go and you got pushed back against a man.

I believe that this phenomenon of domineering women is due to a few factors:

The absence of domestic male presence especially in the African-American culture which has bred a dominant black woman and for that I don't blame the black woman. Everybody gives a black woman a bad mark for being as dominant as she is.

Well, what is she to do if our metaphor men are being locked up in jail, killed in the streets … great portion of them now turning homosexual and she's left there with children and those that are not part of those categories make babies and won't commit and she's left there with children and she has to be everything to the child or the children what she's left to do nothing but develop muscles that were never really supposed to be developed.

Some of the misguided objectives of women's liberation where you have a certain women who want to rob the man of his social and psychological role in the family and in the community where you take it so far as to where there's almost no difference between male or female man or woman husband or wife.

A culture that is constantly eliminating the boundaries that define manhood from womanhood. This generates what a generation of women that becomes overly dominant.

It is the will of God for a woman to submit to her husband and so a woman should not marry a man that she cannot submit to. It's as simple as that.

Ephesians chapter 5 verses 22 to 24 says: *"Wives submit yourselves unto your own husband's as unto the Lord. For the husband is the head of the house, even as Christ is the head of the church and he's the savior of the body. Therefore as the church is subject unto Christ, so let the wives be to their own husbands in everything."*

So you know when a man has to fight you to fulfill the role that God has divinely given him, it disconnects him from and breaks the bond of intimacy between you and your husband.

In the book of **Proverbs chapter 21 verses 9:** *"It's better to dwell in a corner of the housetop (meaning on the roof) than with a brawling woman in a wide house."*

It goes without saying that it's better to live on a roof than to live in a mansion with them with a brawling, mean, and domineering woman.

Most wives never take the time to celebrate their husband's greatness instead they get caught up in the common routine of criticism. You can sit there and criticize things about your man and never celebrate the positives.

Many men find themselves in the arms of other women who celebrate them and this often starts out as a survival maneuver to escape the barrage of criticism at home.

You don't want your man going to the job and a woman at the job celebrating his achievements and accomplishments and you're saying nothing.

You need to know that a man needs to be celebrated more in his own house than in the street or church.

Personally, when I come home and I try to do my little best to clean up or whatever errands that needs to be done or better yet, you can as well ask your wife what needs to be done or what you can assist her with.

When your man does that he wants you to approve of he would do everything to get your approval.

Most men want your approval because they are ego-driven and that's just a reality. The wife's approval is what builds the ego of the man.

Your husband needs to know that you celebrating him because even if he may not be Clark Kent but if you celebrate him, you'll turn him into Superman.

You can say something in this line to your husband: "You're a great provider. I want you to know that I love you and you're awesome in trying to lead the family spiritually sound."

Learn to celebrate and approve your husband and he'll be more than willing to do more and show you more care and love. However, when a man comes home to a wife that doesn't celebrate him, there's something that happens in his psyche and way of reasoning.

It goes without saying that too much criticism can rob a man of any sexual desire for a woman and the devil starts giving him all kinds of imaginations in his mind like: "Your wife doesn't love you. She doesn't appreciate you. You're doing all this hardwork in vain."

You get the drift?

And the next step that could happen could be someone else doing what you were supposed to be doing and that's where the problem sets in.

Or how would you explain the fact that you let your man go on the street and other people are celebrating him and when he comes home, you say nothing or just sitting around the house popping gum without saying a word to your husband.

Or when your husband is working two and three jobs to take good care of you and you haven't even said any word of appreciation to him.

In **Proverbs chapter 31 verses 11 to 12**, it says: *"... for the heart of her husband doth safely trust in her so that so that he shall have no need of spoil. She would do him good and not evil all the days of her life."*

And one of the ways you do a man good is to build his self-esteem with your approval. The whole world can tell him he's great and other nice things but if you say nothing, it's horrible and brings doubts to his heart about if truly those things are true which could affect his personality and confidence.

The man gets disgusted with his wife when she keeps a filthy home and get this straight: this is no woman's job but when you look into the book of Genesis, in the garden of Eden, God ordained Adam to keep the garden and we looked at Garden of Eden was his home and it meant to be kept well and organized.

In true reality, the whole family is the reflection of the quality of the woman while the well-being of the family is a reflection of the quality of the man.

What I mean is that, if a family is starving and there's an able-bodied man in the house calling himself dad and husband, the world will say it's a shame that the man is not taking care of his family financially.

However, if the same world comes to your house and your house is filthy, they're going to leave with a sense of shame of how filthy that woman got her family living in a house that filthy because the condition of the home is the reflection of the woman.

I believe that men can help out around the house as well but I believe if you are a woman and you are a mother, a nurturer, and one that protects and cares and organizes, there's no way in the world you would have your family in a filthy house.

When this happens, one of the husbands complaint would definitely be that you keep a filthy house especially if he's working and you're at home all day and this man comes back home to a filthy house: all the Mac makeup littered everywhere and you've all that trash on your floor.

I've gone to some houses and I don't even know how some people even invite folk to come up in a house that's just so full of shit.

There's no way you would offer me food that I'll accept because of the impression from the way your home is unkept. It would generally send the message that if your house is very filthy, there is more likelihood that your food would not be hygienic.

And that's exactly what the Bible says in **Titus 2 verses 3 to 5**: *"The aged women likewise, that they be in behavior as becometh holiness, not false accusers, not given to much wine, teachers of good things. That they may teach the young women to be sober, to love their husbands, to love their children, to be discreet, chaste, keepers at home, good, obedient to their husbands, that the word of God be not blasphemed."*

How are you going to be somebody's wife and you don't know how to clean the house.

Obviously, men should also assist in the house chores as well but it's a reflection on womanhood when you can just walk around a nasty filthy house all day long and got a family up in there and also got children in the filthy house.

In **Proverbs 31**, *"a good woman looketh well to the ways of her household and eateth not the bread of idleness."*

Now, this woman here ran businesses, and also had staff. She bought and sold land and goods and she had a wealthy husband but she still salted away and looked well to the ways of her household and I say once more, husband should help wives to do this but the wife should be the driving force behind the condition of that home.

As a husband and father, my mind is consumed with the well-being of my family financially. My wife doesn't have to drive me and that door I want to make sure my family is good.

If I die (God forbid), I don't want my wife worrying about where she's going to find money to take care of herself and maintain her lifestyle.

As you can see that's the man in me. It more like an inbuilt feature which explains why the woman in a wife should say I'm going to have this filth out of my house

and keep it in a good condition as
walk.

3 THINGS EVERY WIFE SHOULD DO FOR HER HUSBAND

I'm going to dive into 3 things that I really believe every wife needs to do for her husband.

However, it goes without saying that everyone is different and there are different situations for different people but what I would be sharing are things that have impacted my marriage if I do them or don't do them.

Obviously, you keep learning in your marriage everyday because no one is a perfect wife but you just need to strive to be the best wife your husband craved for.

Tip Number one: Always Touch Your Husband

I remember growing up even being like four five and six and hanging out at like family functions or church functions or groups or whatever and I'd see a man and a woman and I would just think of them as that and would have no idea they were actually married because they showed no signs of physical affection towards each other.

I would never see them even hug or hold hands or lean into each other even when they sit beside each other.

I would want to encourage you as a wife that absolutely behind closed doors touch your husband because I really do think it's important to have an intimate physical relationship with your husband.

Of course, you don't necessarily need to go overboard about it especially when you're in public because not everyone is comfortable when it's too intense but things like sitting beside your husband, leaning into your husband, holding your husband's hand, touching your husband …usually goes a long way to crate that bond between the two of you.

It's all very important because guys are huge into physical touch because when you touch your husband in public, you're not just touching him and making him feel good but you're showing everyone around that: "Hey, this is my husband and I am crazy about him" which will give him tons of self-confidence.

There is nothing sweet as being married to a very confident man so I encourage you to always embrace your husband in public.

Tip Number Two: Respect Your Husband

Next, I want to talk about respecting your husband and this is a huge thing that is so key for an awesome marriage relationship. Men need respect more than anything else even love. That's just how they are structured.

Once you start going the opposite direction as a wife and decide not to put your trust in them, it actually means you see your husband as being incapable and belittled.

With this, you're going to find your husband being absolutely defeated and trust me you don't want to be married to a defeated man because that is a horrible feeling that affects you and also affects your kids if you have them.

It goes without saying that it'll affects your husband will make him go ahead second-guessing a lot of things that don't need to be second-guessed.

He's supposed to have full confidence knowing that his wife really respects him and come to realize his roles as a husband.

Wives respect your husband. Wives respect your husband. I'm resounding this so it gets ingrained into your head.

Aside the fact that it's biblical, the reward is just amazing because the more respect you give to your husband, the more affection and joy you would get from him as well.

You need to be your husband's confidant just like they are supposed to be as well.

So, don't spill their emotions because there would come a time when your husband would need to talk to you or just vent regarding something on his mind.

Don't try to argue with him on that occasion because that's a recipe for more issues instead just listen and say okay or further help him out if you really feel like he needs it.

And whatever he tells you is not to be shared amongst your girlfriends, your mother, or anybody for that matter because he needs to know that his heart, what's on his mind and his secrets are safe with you.

The more you have this attitude towards your husband kind of pouring himself out and venting himself to you the more he'll be willing to do it and the more trust and security he'll put into you and that is just a huge blessing and something really exciting for a wife to have in her husband.

Tip Number Three: Know Your Husband's Love Language

You've to know what your husband's love language is and feed it. When I first got married to my wife, she knew my love language was physical touch and closeness.

But her love language wasn't physical touch up till today. When I pass, she always touches me or when I'm sitting on the couch and she has some free time, she would come and sit close to me.

Or if we're just walking side by side, she always holds me by the hand and this really makes me go crazy.

There are several love languages but I encourage you to find your husband's love language and absolutely fuel it on an everyday basis.

DROP AN HONEST REVIEW FOR THIS BOOK?

I'm curious and I'll love a feedback from you:

- How did this book deliver on its promises?

- And what kind of doubts did you have before starting to read this book?

Simply let me know by leaving an honest review on Amazon. I love getting feedback from readers in order to serve you better.

Emmanuel Aniekan

Here is the direct link

Even if it's a few lines, I'll really appreciate it!

Reviews are very important on Amazon as they speak volume of how the book delivered, shows social proof and give others an idea of the content of the book.

So, if you benefited from this book: **drop a review today** by following this link.

Thank you, I wish you success in all your endeavors.

Printed in Great Britain
by Amazon